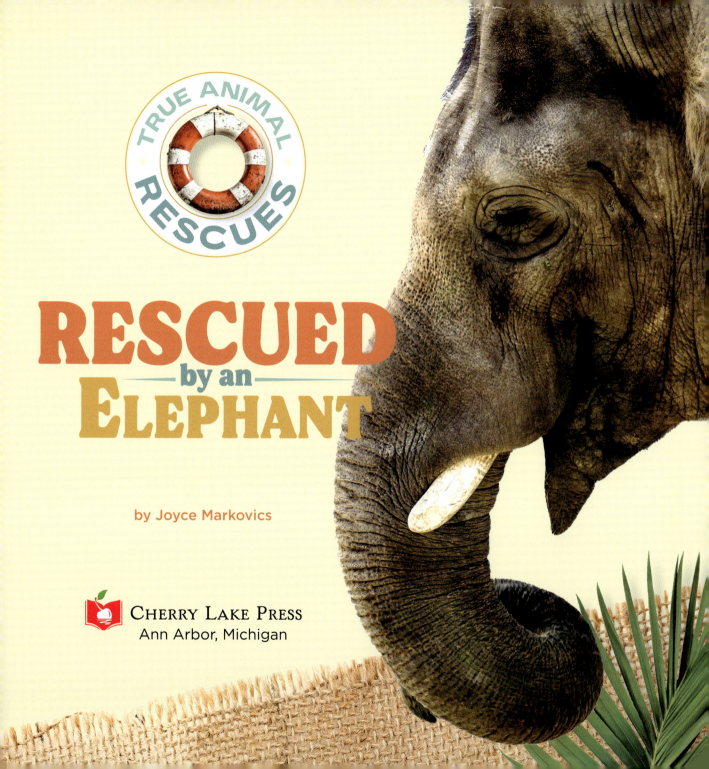

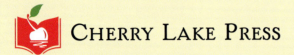

Published in the United States of America by Cherry Lake Publishing
Ann Arbor, Michigan
www.cherrylakepublishing.com

Reading Adviser: Beth Walker Gambro, MS Ed., Reading Consultant, Yorkville, IL

Book Designer: Ed Morgan
Book Developer: Bowerbird Books

Photo Credits: © inigocia/Shutterstock, cover; freepik.com, title page and table of contents; © tonton/Shutterstock, 4-5; freepik.com, 6; © SAHAN SVITLANA/Shutterstock, 7; © Adansijav Official/Shutterstock, 8 and 9; © Nattawut Komvan/Shutterstock, 10; © John Robertson/Telegraph Media Group Holdings Limited 2025, 11 top; freepik.com, 11 bottom; © Manoej Paateel/Shutterstock, 12-13; © Sergey Uryadnikov/Shutterstock, 14-15; © Oriol Querol/Shutterstock, 17; freepik.com, 18 bottom; © boivin nicolas/Shutterstock, 18-19; © Mike Dexter/Shutterstock, 20-21.

Copyright © 2026 by Cherry Lake Publishing Group

All rights reserved. No part of this book may be reproduced or utilized in any form or by any means without written permission from the publisher.

Cherry Lake Press is an imprint of Cherry Lake Publishing Group.

Library of Congress Cataloging-in-Publication Data has been filed and is available at catalog.loc.gov.

Printed in the United States of America

Note from publisher: Websites change regularly, and their future contents are outside of our control. Supervise children when conducting any recommended online searches for extended learning opportunities.

Contents

Ning Nong and Amber	4
Protecting Ahana	12
Helping a Friend	16
Incredible Elephants	20
Profile: Elephant Rescuers	22
Glossary	23
Find Out More	24
Index	24
About the Author	24

Ning Nong and Amber

Amber Owen won't soon forget December 2004. She and her family were on vacation in sunny Thailand. Their hotel was steps from the beach. Amber, who was 8 at the time, couldn't wait to splash in the sea. "I wanted to learn how to swim," she said. But then something caught her attention from her hotel room. Right there on the beach was a young elephant and his **mahout**. Amber rushed to get a closer look. The elephant, she learned, was named Ning Nong.

Elephants are a popular attraction in Thailand. They can be trained to walk with people on beaches and give them rides.

Amber was excited to see Ning Nong up close. However, she stood quietly by his side. Other children swarmed the big animal. Suddenly, Ning Nong gently grabbed Amber's arm with his trunk. Amber's heart leapt with joy.

Every day after that, Amber visited Ning Nong. She fed him bananas. And Amber learned to ride him with the help of the mahout. They rode up and down the beach and into the water. Amber and Ning Nong's friendship grew. "He would wrap his trunk around my shoulders and nuzzle me," said Amber. Little did she know what was about to happen days later.

Bananas are a sweet treat for elephants.

A young girl like Amber riding an elephant on a beach

On the morning of December 26, Amber was riding Ning Nong on the beach. But something wasn't right. "I could tell he was **anxious** and kept turning away from the sea," she said. What Amber didn't know was that a huge earthquake had struck offshore. It triggered a tsunami. Ning Nong started running toward land. Amber tightly clutched his back.

During the first sign of a tsunami, water pulls back from shore. This helps make the tsunami waves stronger.

A tsunami (soo-NAH-mee) is a group of long waves that often causes a lot of destruction. Tsunamis are usually caused by underwater earthquakes.

A huge wave swept over the beach. It reached the elephant's shoulders. He kept running. "He knew something was wrong," said Amber. Around them, the **surging** water swallowed up trees and small houses. Amber watched people being swept out to sea.

After the earthquake, waves flooded the land. They swept away buildings, cars, and people. It's thought around 300,000 died.

With all his might, Ning Nong pushed forward. Water whirled around him. But he remained on his feet. The elephant finally reached a high wall. He wedged himself against it so Amber could climb to safety. "I remember being so scared but so relieved," she said.

Elephants are strong swimmers. They can swim for long distances and use their trunks as snorkels!

Minutes later, Amber's family found her on the wall. Together, they raced to higher ground. "The elephant saved her," said Amber's mom. "He knew the signs that something bad was going to happen and carried me to safety," Amber added. "I thank him for my life."

Amber Owen as an adult

Protecting Ahana

Amber is not the only young person who was saved by an elephant. In 2019, a family of three was riding their scooter in India. Nitu and his wife, Titli, and their 4-year-old daughter, Ahana, had just visited a **temple**. The area was near a dense forest. On their way home, a herd of elephants **emerged** from the forest. The giants walked onto the road.

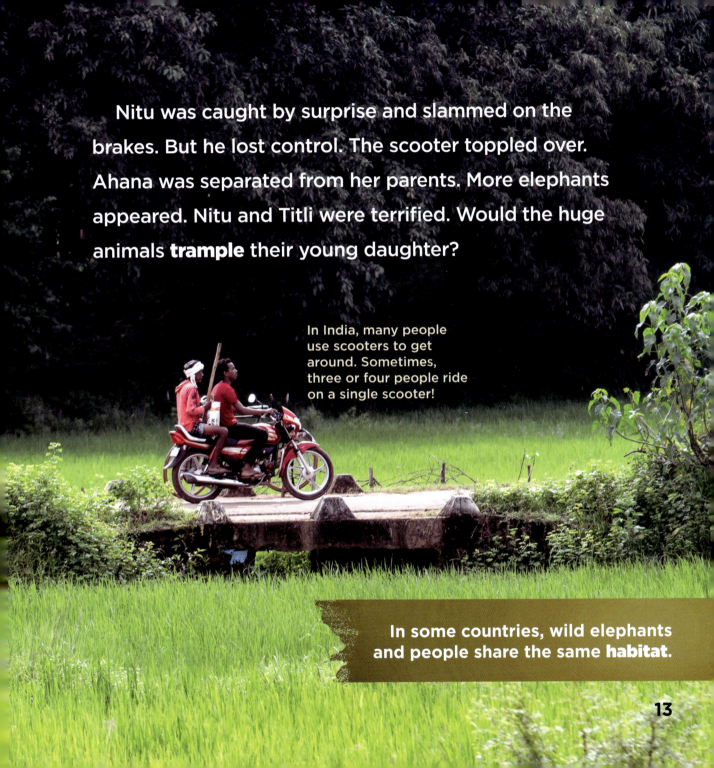

Nitu was caught by surprise and slammed on the brakes. But he lost control. The scooter toppled over. Ahana was separated from her parents. More elephants appeared. Nitu and Titli were terrified. Would the huge animals **trample** their young daughter?

In India, many people use scooters to get around. Sometimes, three or four people ride on a single scooter!

In some countries, wild elephants and people share the same **habitat**.

When Nitu and Titli looked up, they were amazed. One of the elephants was standing over their daughter. Ahana was safe between its front legs. That elephant seemed to be protecting the small child from the other herd members. Once the herd was back in the forest, Ahana's elephant joined them. Nitu and Titli grabbed their daughter and hugged her tightly. They were thankful to Ahana's elephant **guardian**.

Nitu and Titli had minor injuries from the accident. But Ahana was unhurt.

Elephants sometimes travel on roads used by people. These large animals can get into accidents with cars and other vehicles.

Helping a Friend

Another elephant guardian is Kham La. She was born in **captivity** in Thailand. Her owners abused her and her mother. Then Darrick Thomson came to their rescue. Darrick works at an elephant **sanctuary**. From the moment they met, Darrick and Kham La clicked. "We have a very close, special bond," he said.

Over time, their bond grew stronger. Whenever they're together, Kham La holds Darrick's hand with her trunk. And when he calls for her, she runs to him like a pet dog.

The Elephant Nature Park in Thailand where Darrick works

One day, Darrick went for a swim in the river at the sanctuary. Kham La and some other elephants were nearby. Darrick started splashing in the water and making loud noises. Kham La immediately looked up. She thought her friend needed help. So, she rushed into the water to "save" him! The elephant wrapped her trunk around her friend's **torso**. Then she pulled Darrick back to shore.

Elephants have been known to rescue other animals, including baby rhinos!

Elephants bathe in the same river where Darrick went for a swim.

Incredible Elephants

Darrick wasn't entirely surprised by Kham La's brave feat. From working with her and other elephants, he knows how amazing these animals are. Darrick also knows elephants need protecting. "There're too many of us and little left of their habitat," said Darrick. He hopes more people will take action to save elephants and the places where they live.

"There's a lot to learn from animals, especially elephants," he said. Darrick deeply believes in the sanctuary's message: Treat animals with love, and they will love us back.

Without more protection, elephants could become **extinct** in the near future.

PROFILE: Elephant Rescuers

Why do some elephants rescue and protect people? Here are some amazing elephant qualities that could explain why.

Kind
Elephants are known for being kind. If a calf is lost, for example, elephants will help reunite the baby with its mother. They will also comfort it with gentle sounds and touches.

Intelligent
Elephants make and use tools, such as branches, to swat bugs. They can also solve puzzles and remember hundreds of different faces!

Compassionate
If an elephant is hurt or in distress, other elephants will help care for it. They will also feed a sick member of their herd.

Glossary

anxious (ANGK-shuhs)
worried

captivity (kap-TIV-uh-tee)
a place where an animal lives that is not its natural home, and it is not free

emerged (ih-MURJD)
came out from somewhere hidden

extinct (ek-STINGKT)
when an animal has died out

guardian (GAR-dee-uhn)
a protector

habitat (HAB-uh-tat)
a place in nature where an animal lives

mahout (muh-HOWT)
a person who works with and cares for an elephant

sanctuary (SANGK-choo-air-ee)
a place in nature where animals are cared for and protected

surging (SURJ-ing)
moving powerfully and suddenly

temple (TEM-puhl)
a building used for worship

torso (TOR-soh)
the middle part of the human body

trample (TRAM-puhl)
to crush something by walking on it

Find Out More

BOOKS
125 Animals That Changed the World. Washington, DC: National Geographic Kids, 2019.
Markovics, Joyce. *Amazing Animal Minds: Elephants*. Ann Arbor, MI: Cherry Lake Press, 2024.
Recio, Belinda. *When Animals Rescue*. New York, NY: Skyhorse Publishing, 2021.

WEBSITES
Explore these online sources with an adult:

Britannica Kids: Elephant

PBS: Soul of an Elephant

Wild Kratts: Elephant Brains

Index

accident, 13–15
Ahana, 12–15
earthquake, 8–9
elephants, wild, 13–15
extinction, 21
flooding, 9
habitat, 13, 20
India, 12–13
Kham La the elephant, 16–20
mahout, 4, 6
Ning Nong the elephant, 4–11
Nitu, 12–14
Owen, Amber, 4–12
sanctuary, 16, 18, 21
scooter, 12–13
Thailand, 4–5, 16–17
Thomson, Darrick, 16–21
Titli, 12–14
tsunami, 8–11

About the Author

Joyce Markovics is drawn to stories that tug at her heart. When she's not writing books for kids, she volunteers at an animal sanctuary where dozens of different species peacefully coexist. Joyce dedicates this book to Gene Fleming, who's as wise as an elephant.